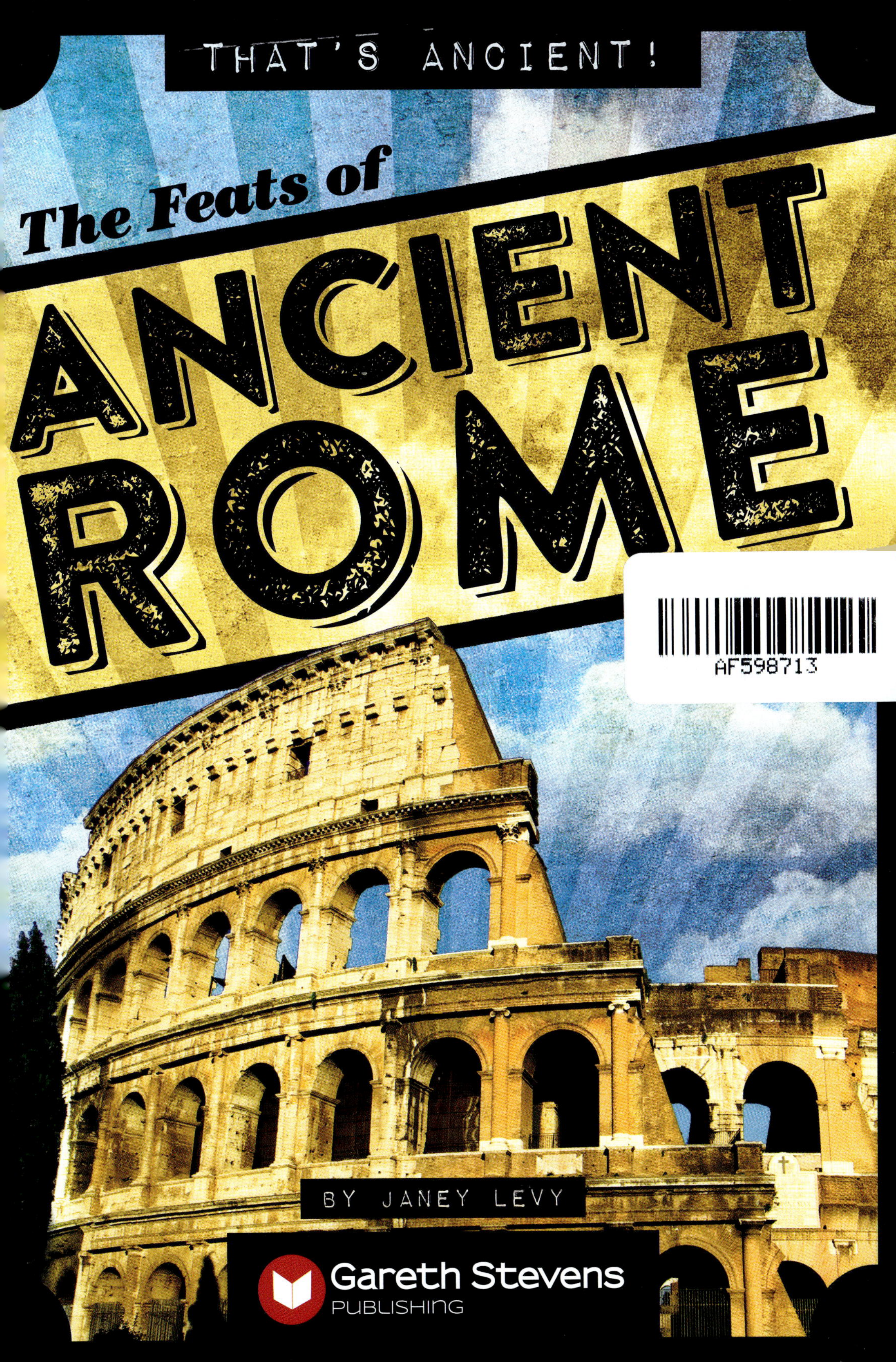
THAT'S ANCIENT!
The Feats of
ANCIENT
ROME
AF598713
BY JANEY LEVY
Gareth Stevens
PUBLISHING

Please visit our website, www.garethstevens.com. For a free color catalog of all our high-quality books, call toll free 1-800-542-2595 or fax 1-877-542-2596.

Library of Congress Cataloging-in-Publication Data

Names: Levy, Janey, author.
Title: The feats of ancient Rome / Janey Levy.
Description: New York : Gareth Stevens Publishing, [2022] | Series: That's ancient! | Includes index.
Identifiers: LCCN 2020045710 (print) | LCCN 2020045711 (ebook) | ISBN 9781538265710 (library binding) | ISBN 9781538265697 (paperback) | ISBN 9781538265703 (set) | ISBN 9781538265727 (ebook)
Subjects: LCSH: Rome—Civilization—Juvenile literature. | Civilization, Western—Roman influences—Juvenile literature. | Rome—History—Juvenile literature.
Classification: LCC DG77 .L48 2022 (print) | LCC DG77 (ebook) | DDC 937—dc23
LC record available at https://lccn.loc.gov/2020045710
LC ebook record available at https://lccn.loc.gov/2020045711

First Edition

Published in 2022 by
Gareth Stevens Publishing
29 E. 21st Street
New York, NY 10010

Designer: Katelyn E. Reynolds
Editor: Therese Shea

Photo credits: Cover, p. 1 SAKhanPhotography/Shutterstock.com; cover, pp. 1–32 (burst) Dawid Lech/Shutterstock.com; cover, pp. 1–32 (clouds) javarman/Shutterstock.com; p. 5 Andrei Minsk/Shutterstock.com; p. 7 (inset) Shakko/Wikipedia.org; pp. 7, 14 Carlo Hermann/AFP via Getty Images; pp. 9, 11 (inset) Andreas Solaro/AFP via Getty Images; p. 9 (inset) Nashvilleneighbor~commonswiki/Wikimedia.org; pp. 10, 11, 15 Filippo Monteforte/AFP via Getty Images; p. 10 (inset) Alberto Pizzoli/AFP via Getty Images; p. 13 joserpizarro/Shutterstock.com; p. 17 Joseph Eid/AFP via Getty Images; p. 19 poludziber/Shutterstock.com; p. 21 MonikaKL/Shutterstock.com; p. 23 Sean Gallup/Getty Images; p. 23 (inset) Fine Art Images/Heritage Images/Getty Images; p. 25 Strawberry Blossom/Shutterstock.com; p. 27 (left) Ratte/Wikipedia .org; p. 27 (right) Hulton Archive/Getty Images; p. 29 (clock) 24Novembers/Shutterstock.com; p. 29 (scalpel) ADragan/Shutterstock.com; p. 29 (mail) Quang Ho/Shutterstock.com.

Printed in the United States of America

Some of the images in this book illustrate individuals who are models. The depictions do not imply actual situations or events.

CPSIA compliance information: Batch #CWGS22: For further information, contact Gareth Stevens, New York, New York, at 1-800-542-2595.

CONTENTS

Words in the glossary appear in **bold** type the first time they are used in the text.

Ancient

Today, Rome is the capital of Italy and an exciting place to visit. Among the sights you'll see are traces of Rome's past. In ancient times, Rome controlled a vast empire.

Not many facts are known about Rome until around 280 BCE, when it was finishing its conquest of Italy. Its empire began in 27 BCE and lasted until 476 CE. Rome is famous for its empire, of course. But that's not all it's famous for.

Many Roman inventions and discoveries have shaped Western civilization. You may not realize it, but we owe our 26-letter alphabet to the ancient Romans. We also owe the form of our calendar to them. Read on to learn about many more achievements and **innovations** of ancient Rome.

THAT'S FASCINATING!

Rome was originally just a small town on the Tiber River in central Italy. Italy at that time was home to many cultures and languages.

ROMAN EMPIRE IN 117 CE

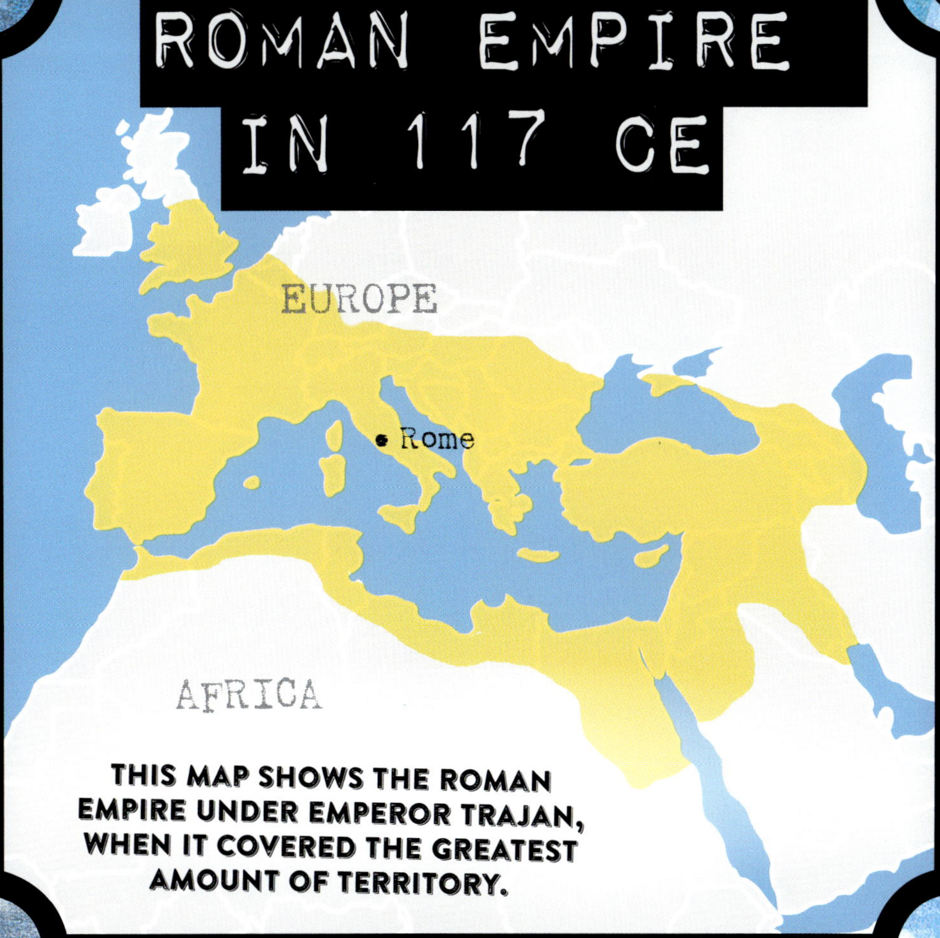

EUROPE

Rome

AFRICA

THIS MAP SHOWS THE ROMAN EMPIRE UNDER EMPEROR TRAJAN, WHEN IT COVERED THE GREATEST AMOUNT OF TERRITORY.

The Etruscans

The Etruscans (ee-TRUHS-kuhnz) were Italy's first highly civilized people. Their home was north of Rome, and they had a great trading and farming civilization. They ruled Rome for over a century (616 BCE to 510 BCE). Ancient Romans borrowed many Etruscan practices. They adapted the Etruscan alphabet. Leaders of the Roman Republic adapted their official symbols from the Etruscans. And the tradition of gladiatorial combats—so closely linked to Rome in the popular imagination—actually came from the Etruscans.

The Face of ANCIENT ROME

The ancient Romans were great admirers of the ancient Greeks. After their conquest of Greece in 146 BCE, they took Greek artworks back to Rome. They also commissioned copies of earlier famous Greek artworks. But that doesn't mean Roman art looked just like Greek art. Ancient Roman art had its own distinctive qualities.

One of the most striking qualities of Roman art was its realism. Greek art presented ideal images of people. But Roman art of the time often presented people with wrinkles and big noses and ears. Each person shown was a specific individual, and there was no attempt to make a person look perfect.

These ancient Roman portraits showed people you might expect, such as emperors and other important individuals. They also showed ancestors because, in addition to gods and goddesses, ancient Romans worshipped their ancestors.

THAT'S FASCINATING!

Ancient Romans had a shrine in their home where they kept statues or pictures of their ancestors. It was important to honor their ancestors daily.

THIS SHOWS THE REALISM OF MANY ANCIENT ROMAN PORTRAITS. THIS KIND OF PORTRAIT, WHICH SHOWS THE HEAD AND PART OF THE SHOULDERS, IS CALLED A BUST.

More Roman Art Forms

Sculpture certainly wasn't the only Roman art form. The insides of Roman public and private buildings were often covered with frescoes and **mosaics**. Fresco subjects included portraits, stories about the gods and goddesses, **architecture**, and nature scenes. The architecture and nature scenes were often meant to fool the eye and make it appear you were looking at actual architecture or nature, not painted scenes. Mosaic subjects included portraits, stories about the gods and goddesses, gladiator contests, sports, hunting, history, and nature.

Building the Urban ENVIRONMENT

Take a look around at your city or town. You probably see lots of concrete. There are likely plenty of apartments; you may live in one. Some buildings may have arches or **domes**. Your city or town is probably laid out on a **grid** plan. Most buildings have **central heating**. Maybe you never stopped to think about these things before, but you can thank the ancient Romans for all of them.

Concrete made the rest of Roman building achievements possible, so it's the place to start. As with most Roman innovations, ancient Romans didn't invent concrete. Some form of concrete had existed for thousands of years before the Romans came along. But the Romans developed a superior concrete that allowed them to build structures that still stand 2,000 years later!

THAT'S FASCINATING!

Roman concrete—or, as they called it, *opus caementicium*—was made of lime, water, volcanic rocks called tuff, and volcanic ash called pozzolana. The pozzolana was the magic ingredient.

THE PANTHEON (BELOW), WHICH HONORS ALL THE ROMAN GODS AND GODDESSES, IS ONE OF THE MOST FAMOUS SURVIVING ANCIENT ROMAN BUILDINGS. THE MAIN BUILDING WAS CONSTRUCTED OF CONCRETE AND BRICK. THE PORCH IN FRONT, WITH THE COLUMNS AND TRIANGLE-SHAPED PEDIMENT ABOVE, WAS BUILT OF MARBLE AND GRANITE.

Apartment Living

Apartment buildings (above right), or *insulae*, were a way to deal with Rome's swelling population. They were constructed of bricks covered with concrete or of wood and cheaply built. Businesses often occupied the ground floor. Roman pumping devices could get water only to the lower apartments, so people above those lacked a water supply. They had to carry their water up. They could pay to use public toilets or use **chamber pots**, the contents of which they dumped out the window onto the street below!

Besides concrete, one of the most important features of Roman architecture was the arch. Now, just as with concrete, Romans didn't invent arches—arches had been around for centuries. But Romans were the first to place an arch so that each end rested on a pillar. Big deal, you say? It was, structurally. This way, the arch directs the weight above it out and down to the pillars and the ground below. This means it can carry a much greater load than a horizontal beam.

Once the Romans placed arches on pillars, they could build all sorts of large public structures, which became major features of the Roman Empire. Those structures included bridges, monuments, **amphitheaters**, and **aqueducts**. Aqueducts were immensely important to Roman life, and you'll read more about them in the next chapter.

THIS IS THE COLOSSEUM IN ROME, THE MOST FAMOUS AMPHITHEATER OF THE ROMAN EMPIRE. CONSTRUCTION BEGAN AROUND 70 CE AND WAS COMPLETED IN 82 CE. IT HAD ARCHES AND BARREL VAULTS, WHICH ARE BASICALLY JUST VERY LONG ARCHES.

THAT'S FASCINATING!

One type of monument Romans liked to build was the enormous triumphal arch. Triumphal arches celebrated military victories and other important events and were commonly decorated with sculpture and writing.

The Arch's Offspring

The dome is an architectural structure that grew out of the arch. As with so many other things, Romans didn't invent domes. But they were the first to use large-scale stone or concrete domes. The most famous Roman dome is that of the Pantheon (above). This dome, made of concrete, rises 142 feet (43 m) above the floor. At the center top of the dome is an opening, called an oculus, which lets in light and air.

Using architectural tools such as concrete, arches, and domes, ancient Romans built their cities. Those cities contained the types of structures you've read about: places for people to live (such as apartment buildings and individual homes for the wealthy), different kinds of public buildings, monuments, amphitheaters, aqueducts, and more. But structures weren't just erected around the city in some sort of aimless way. Ancient Romans used a clever way to organize their cities.

Romans laid their cities out on a grid, just like Roman military camps. The two main streets crossed each other at right angles at the grid's center. Other streets ran parallel to those streets. Romans didn't invent the grid plan, but they took the plan to a new level and made it common.

Heating the Home

Ancient Romans were innovative in heating their dwellings—at least wealthy dwellings. Apartment residents built fires for warmth, creating smoke-filled apartments. However, a central heating system called a hypocaust would warm a wealthy Roman's *domus*, or house. A fire or furnace below a structure sent hot air through spaces below the floor and, often, in the walls. Heat radiated, or spread, from the floor and walls into the room. There were no smoke-filled rooms because the air and smoke rose up through the walls and into the outside air.

IN THIS MODEL OF A ROMAN CITY, YOU CAN SEE HOW THE STREETS ARE LAID OUT IN REGULAR FASHION AND CROSS EACH OTHER AT RIGHT ANGLES.

THAT'S FASCINATING!

The practice of laying out cities on a grid plan—so widely used across the Roman Empire—was never applied to Rome itself! Two factors made it difficult. There was a long tradition of Roman leaders building new structures wherever they pleased, and the city was spread across several hills, which made a grid challenging.

Water

Remember the aqueducts mentioned in the previous chapter? It's time to get back to those. They were critically important to life in the ancient Roman world.

Using gravity, aqueducts carried freshwater to city centers from surrounding hills and mountains. This meant Roman cities had ample water to meet their needs—drinking, cooking, washing, and **sanitation**. Public health was promoted. Cities grew large. Rome's population, for example, exceeded 1 million at the beginning of the Roman Empire. No city would have that many people again for over 1,000 years!

One major use of water was bathing. Private homes of the wealthy might have their own baths. But Romans frequently visited quite splendid public baths. These were not simply places to get clean; they were places to relax and socialize.

THIS IS THE INSIDE OF ONE PART OF THE PUBLIC BATHS IN THE ANCIENT ROMAN CITY OF POMPEII (PAHM-PAY).

THAT'S FASCINATING!

As with the arches Romans used to build them, aqueducts weren't invented by Romans. The first Roman aqueducts were built around 312 BCE, hundreds of years after the earliest aqueducts appeared.

More About Roman Baths

You probably don't consider bathing a social occasion. But it might help to think of Roman baths as spas, or places devoted to health and relaxation. There was an exercise room, hot room, steam room, warm room, and cold room, which usually had a swimming pool. A hypocaust heated the hot room and sometimes the warm room too. There was someone to rub special oils on bathers and even to massage their muscles to relax them. There were also gardens and club rooms!

Another major use of water in Roman cities was sanitation. You might be surprised to learn ancient Romans had flush toilets. However, those toilets were *nothing* like modern flush toilets.

Most Romans used public bathrooms, and privacy wasn't exactly a concern there. Public bathrooms consisted of rooms with long stone benches that had holes in them every few feet for people to sit over. Flowing water ran below the benches to carry away—or flush—the waste. The waste was carried into the **sewer** system and then into the nearest river—not exactly an environmentally friendly solution.

Ancient Romans didn't have toilet paper. So how did they clean themselves after going to the bathroom? They used a sponge on a stick—which was shared with everyone. Eww!

Home Toilets

In case you're wondering, some people did have toilets at home. But the arrangement probably wasn't what you're expecting. The toilet was near or even *in* the kitchen. Why? People also used it to dispose of food scraps. Home toilets weren't connected to the sewer system. People were afraid of sewer rats crawling into their home. That meant the toilet had to be cleaned out periodically by hand. Yuck! The contents were probably dumped into gardens or fields outside the town.

AS WITH SO MANY OTHER CELEBRATED FEATURES OF ROMAN CIVILIZATION, FLUSH TOILETS WEREN'T INVENTED BY ROMANS. THEY'D BEEN AROUND FOR THOUSANDS OF YEARS. BUT THE ROMANS ADOPTED THEM MORE WIDELY THAN ANYONE BEFORE THEM.

THAT'S FASCINATING!

Ancient Romans faced a rather unpleasant problem with their public toilets. The gases from the waste sometimes caused fires to erupt through the holes!

All Roads Lead TO ROME

Helping the growth and effective functioning of the Roman Empire were the Roman roads. It probably goes without saying at this point that Romans didn't invent roads. Roads had existed for thousands of years. But Romans developed roads far beyond what anyone had before, and they built such amazing roads that some survive today!

Romans wanted the shortest distance between points, so Roman roads are famously straight. And it took a lot of work to create these straight roads. Romans drained marshes, cut through forests, cut into mountainsides, and tunneled through mountains.

Travel on these straight roads was fast and easy. And Romans were among the first to use mile markers and road signs telling travelers how far to the next town. Soldiers patrolled the roads to keep travelers safe.

THAT'S FASCINATING!

The ancient Romans built over 50,000 miles (80,467 km) of roads. That's more miles than are in the U.S. Interstate Highway System!

MAJOR ROADS WERE AT LEAST 14 FEET (4.2 M) WIDE, WHICH WAS ENOUGH SPACE FOR TWO CARRIAGES TO PASS EACH OTHER.

The Composition of Roman Roads

Roman roads were built in layers. First, a trench was dug where the road would go. The soil was packed down to make it solid and stable. Then a layer of crushed rock was added. Next came a layer of cement and crushed rock. On top of that was a layer of concrete, sand, and gravel. Large blocks of stone formed the top layer. The roads were built higher in the middle than on the sides so that rainwater would run off them.

A, B, C

You learned the alphabet years ago. But did you ever wonder where it came from? You may know several alphabets exist, such as the Arabic and the Greek alphabets. The alphabet you learned—the one being used to form the words you're reading now—is the Latin alphabet. And it comes from the Latin-speaking ancient Romans.

Of course, some differences exist between the ancient Latin alphabet and the modern one. Originally, the Latin alphabet had only 20 letters, not 26 like it does today. It lacked G, J, U, W, Y, and Z. It later added G, Y, and Z, bringing its total to 23.

The earliest known writing in the Latin alphabet comes from the 6th century BCE. At that time, people wrote from left to right *or* from right to left!

THAT'S FASCINATING!

Here's something else about the old Latin alphabet that may surprise you: It had only capital, or uppercase, letters. There were no lowercase letters. EVERYTHING WAS WRITTEN LIKE THIS!

THE ROMANS, OF COURSE, DIDN'T INVENT THEIR ALPHABET OUT OF NOTHING. THEY ADAPTED THE ALPHABET USED BY THE EARLIER ETRUSCAN CIVILIZATION.

A Little Bit of Latin

Latin may seem like a strange and ancient language you don't know anything about. But you'd be surprised. Many English words are based on Latin words. Here are a few examples.

LATIN	MEANING	ENGLISH
alta	tall, high	altitude
magna	great	magnificent
nova	new	novice
prima	first	primary
schola	school	scholar

Read It

HERE FIRST

For many adults, reading a newspaper—either physical or digital—is an important daily tradition. The first printed newspaper appeared in Germany in 1609. But the ancestor of newspapers appeared almost 1,700 years earlier in Rome.

Ancient Romans got their news from a government publication called the *Acta Diurna*, or "Daily Events." The *Acta Diurna* was posted at public places around Rome for people to read. Individuals could buy a copy from a **scribe**. And the wealthy could have it delivered to their home.

So what could Romans read in the *Acta Diurna*? Topics included crimes; trials; announcements of military victories; the price of grain; notable births, deaths, and marriages; gladiatorial combats; a gossip column; human interest stories, such as a lost dog finding its way home; and astrological readings!

THAT'S FASCINATING!

All the news in the *Acta Diurna* came from the government and was what the government wanted people to know. No independent news sources existed back then.

THE ROMAN FORUM (BELOW) IS ONE OF THE PLACES WHERE COPIES OF THE *ACTA DIURNA* WOULD HAVE BEEN POSTED. THE FORUM WAS THE RELIGIOUS, LEGAL, AND COMMERCIAL HEART OF ANCIENT ROME.

More About the *Acta Diurna*

Although the content of the *Acta Diurna* was quite similar to that of a modern printed newspaper, it wasn't printed. Printing hadn't been invented, and the ancient Romans didn't have paper! The *Acta Diurna* was a handwritten newssheet. No copies of the *Acta Diurna* have survived, so we don't know what it was written on. It seems likely it was written on a form of papyrus or maybe stone or metal. Perhaps it looked somewhat like the image above.

Aprilis Showers Bring

MAIUS FLOWERS

You know the calendar months and probably know we have a solar calendar, based on how long Earth takes to revolve around the sun. But have you ever wondered where our calendar came from?

The modern Gregorian calendar was adopted in 1582. However, it was closely based on the ancient Roman Julian calendar, which also gave us the names of our months.

The Julian calendar was named after Julius Caesar, who introduced it in 46 BCE to fix the original Roman calendar. The original calendar caused problems because it was shorter than a solar year. The new calendar kept the old calendar's 12 months, but it had 365 days—roughly a solar year. And to keep it on track with the solar year, it added a leap day to February every 4 years.

Solar Calendar Challenges

Basing a calendar on the solar year presents challenges. The solar year is 365 days, 5 hours, 48 minutes, and 46 seconds. But a calendar can't be exactly that long. So the calendar is 365 days, and every 4 years a leap day is added. But since the time over 365 days isn't *quite* one-fourth of a day, adding a full day every 4 years puts the calendar off track with the sun. So elaborate rules determine years when a leap day won't be added, to line things up again.

THESE ARE THE ROMAN NAMES FOR THE MONTHS IN THE ORIGINAL JULIAN CALENDAR. QUINTILIS WAS RENAMED IULIUS IN 44 BCE TO HONOR JULIUS CAESAR. SEXTILIS WAS RENAMED AUGUSTUS IN 8 BCE TO HONOR AUGUSTUS CAESAR. YOU'LL NOTICE THAT THE LETTER I IS USED FOR IANUARIUS, IUNIUS, AND IULIUS INSTEAD OF J. REMEMBER, THERE IS NO J IN LATIN.

IANUARIUS

M	T	W	T	F	S	S
					1	2
3	4	5	6	7	8	9
10	11	12	13	14	15	16
17	18	19	20	21	22	23
24	25	26	27	28	29	30
31						

FEBRUARIUS

M	T	W	T	F	S	S
	1	2	3	4	5	6
7	8	9	10	11	12	13
14	15	16	17	18	19	20
21	22	23	24	25	26	27
28						

MARTIUS

M	T	W	T	F	S	S
	1	2	3	4	5	6
7	8	9	10	11	12	13
14	15	16	17	18	19	20
21	22	23	24	25	26	27
28	29	30	31			

APRILIS

M	T	W	T	F	S	S
				1	2	3
4	5	6	7	8	9	10
11	12	13	14	15	16	17
18	19	20	21	22	23	24
25	26	27	28	29	30	

MAIUS

M	T	W	T	F	S	S
						1
2	3	4	5	6	7	8
9	10	11	12	13	14	15
16	17	18	19	20	21	22
23	24	25	26	27	28	29
30	31					

IUNIUS

M	T	W	T	F	S	S
		1	2	3	4	5
6	7	8	9	10	11	12
13	14	15	16	17	18	19
20	21	22	23	24	25	26
27	28	29	30			

QUINTILIS (IULIUS)

M	T	W	T	F	S	S
				1	2	3
4	5	6	7	8	9	10
11	12	13	14	15	16	17
18	19	20	21	22	23	24
25	26	27	28	29	30	31

SEXTILIS (AUGUSTUS)

M	T	W	T	F	S	S
1	2	3	4	5	6	7
8	9	10	11	12	13	14
15	16	17	18	19	20	21
22	23	24	25	26	27	28
29	30	31				

SEPTEMBER

M	T	W	T	F	S	S
			1	2	3	4
5	6	7	8	9	10	11
12	13	14	15	16	17	18
19	20	21	22	23	24	25
26	27	28	29	30		

OCTOBER

M	T	W	T	F	S	S
					1	2
3	4	5	6	7	8	9
10	11	12	13	14	15	16
17	18	19	20	21	22	23
24	25	26	27	28	29	30
31						

NOVEMBER

M	T	W	T	F	S	S
	1	2	3	4	5	6
7	8	9	10	11	12	13
14	15	16	17	18	19	20
21	22	23	24	25	26	27
28	29	30				

DECEMBER

M	T	W	T	F	S	S
			1	2	3	4
5	6	7	8	9	10	11
12	13	14	15	16	17	18
19	20	21	22	23	24	25
26	27	28	29	30	31	

THAT'S FASCINATING!

Other months were renamed by other emperors, but none of those name changes lasted. The emperor Commodus gave all 12 months names he'd adopted for himself: Amazonius, Invictus, Felix, Pius, Lucius, Aelius, Aurelius, Commodus, Augustus, Herculeus, Romanus, and Exsuperatorius.

Law and ORDER

It might surprise you to learn that ancient Roman legal ideas influence modern law, but they do. For example, just like in many judicial systems now, a Roman accused of a crime had a hearing where a judge decided if sufficient evidence existed for a trial. If a trial occurred, witnesses and evidence were presented, just like today.

The foundation of Roman law was the Twelve Tables, a set of laws created around 450 BCE. Earlier **customary** laws existed, but the Twelve Tables was revolutionary. Laws were no longer simply a matter of custom but would be passed by the government and *written down* to ensure equal treatment for all citizens.

Between 533 CE and 556 CE, Emperor Justinian I created the *Corpus Juris Civilis* to update Roman law. All later Western legal systems borrowed greatly from this work.

THAT'S FASCINATING!

The Twelve Tables covered laws on a wide range of subjects, including property and religion. It also listed punishments for everything from stealing to black magic used for evil purposes!

BELOW LEFT, ROMANS READ THE LAWS OF THE TWELVE TABLES. JUSTINIAN I'S *CORPUS JURIS CIVILIS* TOOK ITS PLACE AND INCLUDED THE IDEA THAT A PERSON ACCUSED OF A CRIME IS INNOCENT UNTIL PROVEN GUILTY.

Empress Theodora's Contributions

Empress Theodora, Justinian's wife, made her own contributions to the *Corpus Juris Civilis*. She made sure some women's rights were protected. If a woman was widowed, the money she brought to the marriage would be returned to her. A husband couldn't assume a major debt unless his wife stated her agreement—twice. Women charged with major crimes were to be guarded by women, who were less likely to hurt them than male guards.

It should be clear by now that ancient Rome was responsible for numerous innovations, many of which have shaped the modern world. But the developments you've read about here are only some of ancient Rome's contributions. There are many more.

Ancient Romans developed Roman numerals, such as I (1), II (2), III (3), IV (4), V (5). You might have seen them in movie titles or books. But we don't use them much anymore; they lack zero, and you can't calculate fractions.

Romans invented many new surgical tools and methods. They created the codex, which is the book as we know it. Earlier literature had been written on clay tablets or scrolls. And there are even more ancient Roman innovations. Check out the next page to learn more.

THAT'S FASCINATING!

The ancient Roman postal service was established by Augustus Caesar, who ruled from 27 BCE to 14 CE. It was for government use only.

MORE ROMAN INNOVATIONS

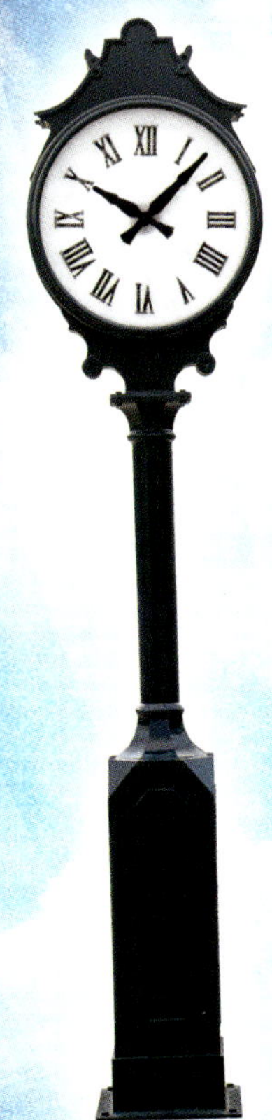

ROMAN NUMERALS

NEW SURGICAL TOOLS AND METHODS

CODEX

LOW-COST FOOD AND CLOTHES FOR THE NEEDY

EDUCATION FOR POOR CHILDREN

POSTAL SERVICE

Surgical Tools and Methods

So what were some of the ancient Roman surgical tools and methods? They had cutting tools called scalpels. They had bone drills and bone saws, which sound kind of scary. They had tools for moving broken bones back into place or removing teeth. Ouch! They had clamps to reduce blood loss. And to help prevent germs from getting into the body during surgery, they soaked their instruments in hot water first.

GLOSSARY

amphitheater: a large, open-air building with seats rising in curved rows around an open space where games and plays take place

aqueduct: a bridge-like structure that is used to carry water across a valley

architecture: the design of buildings

central heating: a system designed to heat all parts of a building

chamber pot: a container that is kept in a bedroom to be used as a toilet

customary: according to custom or tradition rather than written law

dome: a rounded roof

grid: a set of squares formed by crisscrossing lines

innovation: a new way of doing things

mosaic: decoration on a wall, ceiling, or floor made of small pieces of colored glass or stone

sanitation: having to do with actions taken for health and cleanliness

scribe: someone whose job was to copy books and other writings

sewer: a usually underground pipe used to carry away water and waste

FOR MORE INFORMATION

BOOKS

Holland, Simon. *Ancient Rome*. London, UK: Ivy Kids, 2019.

O'Neill, Sean. *50 Things You Didn't Know About Ancient Rome*. Egremont, MA: Red Chair Press, 2020.

WEBSITES

Ancient Rome for Kids
www.ducksters.com/history/ancient_rome.php
Learn about ancient Rome here, and find links to discover even more.

Ancient Rome for Kids
rome.mrdonn.org
Discover more facts about the Roman Empire on this site.

Introduction to Ancient Rome
www.khanacademy.org/humanities/ancient-art-civilizations/roman/beginners-guide-rome/a/introduction-to-ancient-rome
Find out much more about ancient Rome on this website.

INDEX